THE OLD GOLD ROAD

by Graham Craven

Inspired by The Wizard of Oz

Chapter 1 - The Isle of Dosh

Tony is the Head of the Council's Leisure Service. He is responsible for 7 Leisure Centres spread across the city that are all over 20 years old and in need of improvement or refurbishment. They were built at a time when Leisure trends were very different to today and all have multiple squash courts and shallow rectangular swimming pools with no play features. Each Leisure Centre employs a Manager, 3 Assistant Managers and up to 50 other staff as Centre Assistants, Receptionists, Technicians and Cleaners.

The Leisure Service is in decline and costs the Council £5million a year to run. Tony has been told that if he can't stop the decline and start to make a profit that Leisure, a discretionary service, will either be cut or handed over to a private sector Health and Fitness provider that will be able to make a profit.

Tony is passionate about Leisure Services and is desperate to do the right thing by the Council and by the people employed by the Service. Tony has his own ideas on what would make the Service successful but he doesn't know how to go about getting them approved and implementing them. There are plenty of other people with no direct experience in the Leisure industry, like the local Councillors, the Director of Finance and the Marketing Manager, who are all keen to share their views with him on what he needs to do to create a successful business. Their ideas are different to his and this only helps to confuse him even more.

Lacking inspiration and exhausted from spending days drawing up plans only to reject them, Tony falls asleep in front of his PC at home while looking for ideas on the Leisure Wizard web site on the internet. He'd used the Leisure Wizard site before and it had given him plenty of good ideas, but not tonight. Tonight the wise old Wizard, dressed in a dark green suit, who had been Tony's source of inspiration so many times before, had lost his powers. Tony, a keep fit fanatic had promised his dog Ruby that he'd take her for a run on the fields at the back of their house when he'd finished but she knew that it wasn't going to happen tonight. Instead, she gave a sigh of disappointment and flopped to sleep at her master's feet resting her chin on his well worn red trainers.

In no time at all Tony was in a deep sleep and dreaming about running through the fields with Ruby. His dream was so vivid that Tony was unsure whether he was really dreaming or not. In his confusion he found himself running with Ruby along a dusty yellow track which quickly turned into a rocky road which was making him stumble and lose his footing.

It seemed like only minutes ago that they had started running in beautiful sunshine but now they were surrounded by mile upon mile of open countryside with a thick blanket of fog about to settle upon them and make it almost impossible to see where they were going. Just before they were enveloped by the fog Tony caught a glimpse of a rickety wooden road sign which told him that they were a long, long way from civilisation.

The fog became so dense that Tony could barely see beyond the end of his nose. No matter how hard he tried to stay to the rocky road his feet were warning him that he'd strayed onto wet and boggy marshland. He didn't want Ruby to get lost in the fog so he put her on the lead and pulled her close to his side. As he did, he heard a bird screech in the distance and an icy shiver ran down his back as a sudden breeze carried the unlikely sound of people chanting from across the moor. Tony couldn't help himself and found that he was being drawn towards the noise. The chanting grew louder and clearer and Tony knew he must be getting close to the people who were out on the moor. In such a remote place he was a little afraid of whom he might meet but hoped that they would be able to help him find his way back to the road.

Without warning a flash of lightning filled the sky and in that moment Tony saw three old hags chanting and dancing around a steaming black cauldron. The rhythm of their chanting was hypnotic and their wailings beckoned him to move nearer.

> 'Double double toil and trouble, before ye lies a path of rubble
> Sweep aside this rock strewn load, uncover beneath a golden road.
> Before journeys end for red slippered feet, three foul demons ye shall meet.
> Slay each one with wit and nerve and unlock the wisdom ye deserve'.

They repeated the verse over and over before fading into the mist and darkness like a distant memory.

'Wait' called Tony, 'I don't understand what you mean. Where is this road and where will it lead me? And how can I slay three demons armed only with nerve and wit?'

No sooner had the vision of the old hags faded into the fog than the sun came out again. In the distance Tony could see the rickety wooden road sign and was surprised to learn that he hadn't strayed too far from the road after all. He decided that they needed to make their way back to the sign post to help get their bearings again.

As they approached Tony could see that the sign now stood like a scarecrow at the fork of the road. One of its arms pointed to the road that would lead him to Withinreach Hall at Journey's End, home of the great Leisure Wizard, while the other would lead him to the intriguingly named Isle of Dosh. This was a completely different sign post to the one he'd expected and he suddenly felt completely lost. 'Where are we girl?' he said to Ruby who was sniffing the air as if she'd picked up the scent of something tasty to eat, 'and weren't those old hags back there in the fog saying something about Journey's End?'

Before he'd had the chance to collect his thoughts and choose which road to take Tony noticed a flashy electric blue open top sports car racing towards him. 'Only a demon would drive that fast on these country roads,' joked Tony and within seconds the car screeched to a halt beside him spraying rubble all around. When the smoke of burning rubber tyres cleared, he was greeted by Councillor Morgan, the Cabinet Member with responsibility for Sport, Leisure and Tourism.

'Councillor Morgan' said Tony, 'I didn't expect to see you out here but I am so glad that we have. We've lost our way and have no idea which road will take us home. Can you point us in the right direction?'
'I most certainly can' said Councillor Morgan, grinning from ear to ear. Hop in and let me give you a ride for a while'.

Councillor Morgan believes that there's no place for public owned Leisure Centres in the 21st Century and that there are plenty of private gyms in the city if people really want to stay fit. In his view the economy of the city would be better served by providing a different Leisure experience – Casino's, Night Clubs and Fast Food Restaurants.

Councillor Morgan chose the road to the Isle of Dosh and as he drove he took the chance to explain to Tony and Ruby what leisure meant to him. The smell of burgers and fried chicken greeted them long before they got to the Isle of Dosh, making poor Ruby's mouth water. When they got there, Tony could see that this place, with its flashing neon advertisements, perfectly illustrated Councillor Morgan's vision.

Walking through the streets Councillor Morgan was beaming at the crowds of people spending money, enjoying two, three or four drinks and feasting on burgers, deep fried chicken and chips. 'Don't you just love the *ker-chink* of a till' said Councillor Morgan. 'If we heard that noise more often in your Leisure Centres you wouldn't need a subsidy. And I hope you've noticed that some of the profits are put back into the businesses to keep these places looking brand spanking new to keep the punters wanting to come back time after time.

'I'm not sure how many votes you'd get in the next election if our Leisure Centres were serving *punters* with greasy chips, fizzy drinks and alcohol' said Tony, teasing Councillor Morgan, 'but I have taken some ideas from what I've just seen'.

Tony couldn't disagree that things need to be done differently in his Leisure Centres but still believed in his vision that the Council should provide good quality Leisure Centres at a reasonable price for its *customers* and that it should encourage people of all ages to keep fit and enjoy the long term benefits of a healthy lifestyle.

Tony thanked the Councillor for his insight and left him to enjoy the bright city lights and the sound of cash machines registering yet another sale. While Tony hadn't enjoyed the overall experience he had seen that the most successful businesses have been prepared to spend time and money on providing a high level of customer service and keeping their facilities up to date.

With Ruby at his side, Tony jogged back up the road and reflected on what he'd just seen. By the time that they'd reached the old wooden signpost Tony was happy to have left the Isle of Dosh behind and began to think that the Wizard in Withinreach Hall at Journey's End may just hold the answers he's looking for. With this thought in mind he took his first steps on the road to his dreams.

Chapter 1 – The Isle of Dosh	
Learning Outcomes (the learner will)	**Assessment Criteria (the learner can)**
• Understanding the difference between the funding of a Local Authority Leisure Centre and a privately owned Health and Fitness facility.	• Explain the source of public sector funding for Leisure Services. • Describe where a private sector Health and Fitness provider draws its funds from.
• Understand the difference between Revenue and Capital budgets.	• Describe the key features of both Revenue and Capital budgets. • Describe the main causes of expenditure within a leisure facility. • Identify the main sources of income within a leisure facility. • Assess the profit/loss for activities provided within the leisure facility. • Identify the net cost/profit of running a leisure facility from a Revenue Budget Spreadsheet. • Explain the difference between Profit and loss. • Explain the difference between a subsidy and a deficit.
• Understand why the Council run Leisure Centre may have a different Vision to that of the local Health and Fitness provider.	• Explain the vision for the service provided by the Leisure Centre and the Health and Fitness facility. • Describe any differences between the visions of the Council's Leisure Centre and a privately owned Health and Fitness facility. • Explain how the facilities and activities provided help to achieve the vision of both providers.

Activities Linked to Chapter 1

1. Compare the facilities (Gyms, Swimming Pool, Badminton Courts etc.) in a Council run Leisure Centre with a local private sector Health and Fitness provider.
2. Compare the staff structure in a Council run Leisure Centre with that of your chosen Health and Fitness facility. Provide an organisation chart for both. What is the total staff cost of both facilities?
3. Compare the Council's Vision for its Leisure Centres with that of the local Health and Fitness provider. What are the main similarities and differences between them?
4. Compare the activity programme of the Council's Leisure Centre with that of the Health and Fitness facility. List the activities provided for:
   - Toddlers (under 5yrs)
   - Children (5yrs – 15yrs)
   - Adults (16yrs – 50yrs)
   - Older people (over 50yrs)
5. Using annual attendance figures, detail the most popular activities for each age group.
6. Describe how the activities provided help each organisation achieve its Vision.
7. Create a Vision Statement for an imaginary Leisure Service that you are responsible for.

Chapter 2 – Tuppenceworth Moor

As he left the Isle of Dosh behind, Tony started to think about his vision for Leisure Services. It's a very different vision to Councillor Morgan's but there were lessons he could learn from what he'd just seen. Tony was still convinced that plenty of people would share his view of the service but there were still a number of very big hurdles to be crossed if he were to achieve his goal.

Councillor Morgan had shown him that the successful businesses have to spend money on their facilities to give their customers the experience they wanted. Tony knew that his Leisure Centres needed more than just a makeover to be up to date with current trends and attract new customers but where on earth could he find the money to fund his ambitions?

Tony had once picked up the courage to approach Sandra Potts, the fearsome Director of Finance, to ask for more money to run Leisure Services. Sandra's mantra is "essential spends only" and her priority is to balance the Council's budget, a feat which she has achieved for the last ten years no matter how much central government had cut the funding by. On that occasion she simply fixed Tony with an icy stare and said 'you haven't got a business case'. He almost froze on the spot and immediately lost the nerve to argue with her. He walked away knowing that his lack of courage had done nothing to improve the fortunes of Leisure Services.

In recent years there had been an increase in privately owned Health and Fitness Clubs in the city and Tony felt sure that he had lost custom to them. To attract that custom back he knew that he had to modernise his gyms so that they at least offered comparable facilities. But, raising the capital to fund his ambitions would mean having another conversation with Sandra Potts. Or would it?

The prospect of asking the icy Sandra Potts for more money was almost too much to bear for Tony. "I can almost hear what she'll say" he said to Ruby, then, doing his finest impression of Sandra finished the sentence saying "you haven't got a business case". Ruby wasn't worried about business cases, she was just happy to be out running.

Tony had been so lost in thought that he hadn't seen the rickety signpost leaning against the dry stone wall announcing that they were now on Tuppenceworth Moor. So dim were his thoughts that he hadn't even noticed the gloom that they were running in to. The sky had suddenly turned so dark that it wasn't surprising that Ruby hadn't caught sight or scent of the shady character emerging from the gloom like a ghost. She was so startled by his appearance that she was still barking and growling at him as the neatly dressed man introduced himself as Norman Ellis, a Leisure Consultant from a company called 'Fresh Perspectives'.

'Forgive me,' said Norman 'but I couldn't help overhearing the conversation you were having with your dog. There *is* another way to make your dream come true and I'm sure that I can help you. Let's walk and talk.'

Leaving the road, they walked into the moorland taking a route that Norman had obviously used before. The path was well worn to begin with but soon faded into a deep carpet of peat that made walking difficult even for the ever energetic Ruby. It felt to Tony as if he was being watched by unseen creatures lurking in the undergrowth waiting for the right time to grab his ankles and pull him into the boggy ground.

As they walked Norman talked about the need for a brand image, a charging strategy that people could afford to buy into and modern facilities that people would want to use again and again. He spoke with a confidence that Tony wished he could emulate. Norman put this down to experience saying 'don't forget, I've walked down this road before.'

'Three of my Leisure Centres need to be completely redeveloped' explained Tony. 'The other four though aren't too bad and I could think about using the Council's Invest to Save' scheme to upgrade at least one gym every year. The risk with using the Invest to Save scheme though is that I'd have to pay back all the money borrowed from the Council within five years. If I can't make the repayments from the new income I'd hope they'd generate then the Council will simply take the outstanding balance from my revenue account. This could end up closing one or more of my Leisure Centres'.

As they talked Norman suggested using private sector finance as a short cut to achieving Tony's ambitions and said that he could introduce him to all the right people. Norman just laughed when Tony asked if these people would be on the Council's procurement framework.

Norman's voice dropped to a secretive whisper as he went into detail about private sector funding arrangements. It was as if he didn't want the unseen creatures to hear what they were talking about and Tony began to wonder how many of Norman's plans had fallen into the wrong hands and been dragged down into the boggy soggy ground never to see the light of day again.

It all sounded very exciting to Tony but he told Norman of one of his concerns. 'Surely private sector investors will expect to see a return on their investment to keep their shareholders happy. The need for them to make a profit will almost certainly end up costing more than a loan from the Council won't it?' asked Tony. I'd like to have the money to get the work done quickly, thought Tony, but I've still got to demonstrate that any deal represents 'Best Value' for the Council.

'That's absolutely right', said Norman, 'the investors will expect to see a return of their investment but you will be making buckets loads of new income from the customers that will be flocking to use the new facilities in your Leisure Centres. To use your facilities though, we'll expect people to sign up to a membership scheme which locks them into a two year contract whether they use the facilities or not'.
'But what if your plan doesn't work?' asked Tony. 'Your investors would still expect me to repay their loan in full along with any interest. This would be riskier than borrowing the money from the Council.'
'There is no risk' replied Norman, 'I've done this in hundreds of private gyms and I can tweak one of their business cases to let you show Sandra Potts how easy it is to make money'.
'If you are so confident in your plan then I guess you'd be prepared to share the risk with me,' said Tony already starting to negotiate. 'Could we agree that if the new facilities don't make the money you say they will that I won't have to repay the loan at the same level?'
'Absolutely not' said Norman, beginning to sweat. 'The risk stays with the Council and the investors and I get paid regardless of your performance.'
'I don't think Sandra Potts would go along with that,' said Tony, 'and I'm certain that she would no more accept a *'tweaked business case'* than I would. I may not have your experience Mr Ellis but I do know that every business case is unique and I would expect you to have analysed my business before making sweeping

generalisations based on the performance of private sector Health and Fitness Clubs.'

Tony had no idea how he'd found the courage to speak out like this but wasn't finished yet. 'I'm sorry Mr Ellis but I don't think we can do business. It may take me longer to get what I want for my customers but I'd rather know that I've worked out my business case as honestly as possible and can justify every penny I ask for. It's been good to meet you Mr Ellis but I'm going back to the road now to seek out the Leisure Wizard. I'm sure that he'll be able to tell me how to turn my dream for Leisure Services into reality.

'You're making a big mistake son', Norman called out as Tony and Ruby turned and jogged back to the dusty yellow road that had began to look a little less rocky.

'What do you think Sandra Potts would say to private sector funding?' Tony asked Ruby. 'I'm not sure either girl so let's go and find that Wizard and ask him what I should do.'

Chapter 2 – Tuppenceworth Moor	
Learning Outcomes (the learner will)	**Assessment Criteria (the learner can)**
• Understand why a Business Case is needed to justify investment in the business.	• Explain the key components of a Business Case. • Describe the 3 basic business options (Do Nothing, Do the Minimum, Do Something) of any investment. • Describe the Expected Benefits (financial and other) to be derived from a Business Case.
• Have a basic understanding of the Invest to Save concept used by Councils. • Have a basic understanding of the Private Finance Initiative.	• Assess the cost of a given Business Case. • Explain the Return on Investment required to achieve profits or savings. • Calculate the Payback Period required to repay the investment.
• Understand how Risk is assessed and managed within a Business Case.	• Explain the importance of assessing the Risk associated with a Business Case. • Use a simple Risk Matrix to identify the risk associated with a Business Case.

Activities Linked to Chapter 2

1. Compare standard Business Case Templates found through an Internet Search.
2. Complete a Word Search to identify the standard headings found in a Business Case.
3. Visit your local Leisure Centre and identify areas for improvement using capital finance.
4. Consider the risk to a Leisure Centre of converting a Squash Court into a Gym to improve income and attendance levels.
5. Assess the risk of converting a squash court using a standard Risk Matrix.
6. Using the given Business Case calculate how much new income you would have to raise to repay the investment within 5years.
7. Write an original Business Case for an idea to improve one of the facilities in your local Leisure Centre.

Chapter 3 – Shillingsgate

In recent years Tony had seen the cost of running Leisure Services increase and his income levels fall which meant that the Council had to increase the subsidy for the Service every year. He knew that this was an unsustainable position and he'd been told in no uncertain terms that unless things improved some of his Leisure Centres would be closed.

He had spent hours pouring over his revenue accounts. He had brought expenditure under control by meeting Managers on a monthly basis and reinforcing the "essential spend only" message. Income was another thing all together though.

To balance the books to the agreed subsidy level the Leisure Centres had to generate a total income of £2.5million and this was one of the key problems. They simply weren't generating enough income. But, where the accounts gave him a detailed breakdown of the Leisure Centres expenditure, they provided him with very little information about income performance. He had no idea whether all income generating areas were performing badly or if there was a particular problem with gyms, fitness classes or swimming lessons.

To help reduce the subsidy Tony had tried to increase income levels and had opted to hike up his prices in the hope that his existing customers wouldn't mind paying more for the classes they'd attended for years. Unfortunately this strategy had backfired on him and the increased price drove his customers into the arms of his competitors who were offering a wider, much more exciting range of classes at cheaper prices and in newer facilities.

To generate more income Tony had asked his Leisure Centre Managers to promote their activity programmes as widely as possible but was disappointed when they produced clip-art posters on their PC's and only displayed them in the Leisure Centre for existing users to see. In almost every instance the poster advised the reader to 'ask for more details at reception' but all too often when Tony spoke to the reception staff they couldn't tell him any more than was on the poster.

Tony knew that he had to adopt a commercial approach to the marketing of his Leisure Centres but when he had asked the Council's Marketing Manager for help her advice to him had been to use the 3B marketing strategy – Buy a Big Banner – for display on the outside of the Leisure Centres. While he knew that this would be an improvement on the current marketing strategy he was sure that his competitors used more sophisticated approaches.

As they left the bleak open countryside behind them the road gradually became a little smoother and signs of life started to appear. Cottages scattered on distant hillsides looked down on flocks of sheep as they grazed in nearby fields. The number of cottages slowly increased and it wasn't too long before they were greeted by a road sign welcoming them to the small town of Shillingsgate and announcing that today was Market Day.

The market was very busy with shoppers looking for bargains and as he jogged through the village Tony became aware of the number of sales promotion banners, posters and leaflets he was confronted by. There were 'two for the price of one' offers competing with 'free cuddly toy' deals and 'bonus points on selected lines'. Friendly faced sales staff tried to stop him in the street to hand him leaflets promising 'money off' guarantees or to get his contact details to 'enter into a prize draw'. He was even approached by a comic book Super Hero who wanted him to try a new energy drink so that he too could have super powers.

Pauline Carter was the Council's Marketing Manager and was also a keep fit fanatic. She'd had taken up jogging a few years ago to help lose a little excess weight and Tony had helped and encouraged her to meet her goals. Pauline was now an experienced marathon runner and Tony had thought that through her personal enjoyment of exercise she would easily see what he wanted to achieve and would help to make it happen. He couldn't have been more wrong if he'd tried and was completely knocked off balance by Pauline's unwillingness to help. Over time she became one of Tony's personal demons, preferring to undermine his ideas rather than help him meet his aims.

Pauline would often be seen out running and it almost came as no surprise when Tony saw her jogging towards him doing her best to shrug off the approaches made by the sales staff. Think of the Devil and up she pops, thought Tony unkindly.

'Hi, isn't this great?' he called out to Pauline, doing his best to be friendly. 'This is what we need to do in Leisure Services to help meet our income targets.'

As they stood and exchanged pleasantries they were approached by a friendly looking young woman wearing what looked like a Leisure Centre uniform. She smiled as she greeted them and said 'Hi, my name is Lucy and I'm from the local Leisure Centre. I can see that you obviously like to keep fit, so our Early Bird Leisure Membership Scheme may be just up your street. We've even got a special promotion on at the moment for couples who join up together'.
'Oh, we're not a couple' said Tony looking a little embarrassed.
'I'm sorry,' said Lucy, 'in that case I can sign one of you up on our Introduce a Friend promotion so that you can still benefit from a price discount. To become a member all you have to do is fill in a simple form and we'll soon have you achieving all your health and fitness goals. Becoming a member and paying by monthly Direct Debit works out much cheaper than the Pay as You Play option and membership includes a personal fitness plan. You'll also be amongst the first to hear of any new promotions we introduce to help you save money and keep fit at the same time. Is this something that would interest you?'
'I'd love to hear more about your membership scheme but I'm afraid that we're not from around here. We are just passing though' explained Tony.
'That's not a problem', said Lucy. 'I'll give you some leaflets and if you'd like any more details you can look us up on our web site, the address is on the leaflet. You'll also find some special deals for people just like you who might only be able to use our Leisure Centre every now and then. I'll be here for the rest of the day, so don't be afraid to come back and see me later if you'd like any more information. Enjoy the rest of your run'.

Before she left, Lucy handed them both leaflets explaining the range of benefits available to Early Bird Members and gave them other promotional materials, including a pen each with the name, web address and telephone number for the Leisure Centre on it. Everything was branded with the Early Bird logo – a swooping owl with its claws extended – looking like it was set to catch something much more substantial than a worm.

Waiting until Lucy was out of earshot, Tony turned to Pauline and said 'Wow, wasn't she awesome? Did you hear how enthusiastically she spoke about her Leisure Centre and how well informed she was about the promotions they were running? I wish I had staff like her,' he said, remembering how his own staff had floundered when he had asked them for the further information referred to on the posters displayed in his Leisure Centres.

'Look at the promotional materials too Pauline. They do an awful lot more than Buy a Big Banner to attract and retain customers here. We've got to work together to achieve results like these are hit our targets'.

'Your targets,' Pauline corrected him, 'since the marketing budgets were centralised last year, all I have to do is have a balanced budget at year end. And if that means I can't afford to produce the marketing and promotional materials that you'd like then it's just tough, unless of course, you want to pay me more money?'

Tony's blood boiled in an instant but he wasn't prepared to let Pauline see that she had got under his skin. Instead, he responded in kind. 'You know the financial rules, Pauline. I can only give you more money if you can prove you are delivering best value for the Council. Best value doesn't just mean *cheapest.* It means delivering the kind of service that the customer wants and needs in order to do their business. If you can't do this then I will simply look elsewhere and I'm sure that I'll be able to find a Leisure Marketing specialist who is prepared to work with me. Unfortunately for you though, I'll make sure that I get my marketing budget back and you'll just have to work harder to balance your books.'

Pauline was speechless and once again Tony was unsure where he found the nerve to speak out in such a forceful manner like this. 'I'll see you in work where we can carry on this conversation' he said before taking to the road again, only looking back to make sure that Ruby was following him.

As Tony's blood pressure returned to normal he thought again about how impressive Lucy had been in promoting her Leisure Centre and the Early Bird Membership Scheme. She may have been appointed because she had sales skills already thought Tony but someone has done an awful lot of work behind the scenes to make sure that she knew as much as she did about the Membership Scheme and its various promotional packages. To take his mind off Pauline Carter he started to think about the kind of sales training he could provide for his staff.

Chapter 3 – Shillingsgate	
Learning Outcomes (the learner will)	**Assessment Criteria (the learner can)**
• Understand the Marketing Strategies used by Leisure providers to attract new business and retain existing customers.	• Design a marketing promotion to attract new users. • Evaluate the impact of marketing materials on sales performance. • Compare and contrast the promotions used by other commercial organisations with those used by Leisure Providers.
• Understand the sales techniques used by Leisure providers to attract and retain customers.	• Design a Sales Action Plan to achieve monthly sales target. • Conduct a 'Mystery Shopper' telephone survey to evaluate the commitment to customer care of sales staff.
• Understand the financial value of a Membership scheme compared to a 'Pay as You Play' option.	• Assess the income derived from achieving a monthly membership sales target.
• Understand how Sales Targets are set and evaluated.	• Assess past performance to benchmark current performance. • Calculate breakeven costs to determine how many sales are needed to make a profit.

Activities Linked to Chapter 3

1. Compare the prices of the Council's Leisure Centre with those of the Health and Fitness facility.
2. Compare any Pay as You Play prices with the price of a monthly Membership. Which offers best value for money for the customer who wants to use the gym twice per week?
3. Compare the Leisure Centre's Membership Scheme with the Health and Fitness facility. Which scheme offers best value for money?
4. Phone your local Leisure Centre and a local Health and Fitness facility and explain that you are interested in becoming a Member of their gym. Compare their responses and explain which you thought offered the best customer experience.
5. Collect the marketing leaflets and posters from both the Leisure Centre and the Health and Fitness facility. Which is most likely to attract new members? Explain the reasons for your choice.
6. Carry out a newspaper and an Internet search for marketing promotions used by Council Leisure Services and Private Sector Health and Fitness providers. Compare the similarities and differences.
7. Who are the main competitors to the Leisure Centre and the Health and Fitness facility?
8. Carry out a newspaper and Internet Search for marketing promotions used by Supermarkets, Travel Companies and Fast Food Outlets. How do they differ from the promotions being used by the local Leisure Centre and Health and Fitness provider?
9. Devise a promotion for a Leisure Centre designed to attract 40 new members to its gym within 1 month.
10. Design a Sales Action Plan covering a period of 4 weeks showing where you will take you promotion to attract new members for the gym.
11. Produce an Income Spreadsheet to show how much income will be generated by attracting 40 new members to the gym every month for a year. Members pay £20 per month. You should assume that 20% of members will cancel their membership after 3 months.
12. If a Leisure facility fails to meet its sales target, what can it do about it?

Chapter 4 - Meeting the Leisure Wizard

Tony found that he had a new spring in his step as he left Shillingsgate to continue on his journey and his much anticipated meeting with the Leisure Wizard. The road was long and winding and took him high up a mountainside where his vision became obscured by cloud. The cold damp air made his legs ache and the trek to the peak seemed endless. Ruby with her boundless energy was ahead of him making the climb look easy. Tony paused for breath at the top of the mountain and hoped that it wouldn't be too long before even a small amount of sunlight found its way through the cloud to warm him. The weather can change in dramatic fashion in the mountains at this height and it didn't disappoint today. As if making a dramatic entrance in a stage play the sun burst through the clouds in a majestic blaze of glory and evaporated all cloud in an instant.

Looking away from the spectacle in the sky he thought his eyes must be deceiving him when there, in the valley below, stood a magical vision – a vast mansion gleaming gold in the midst of a green landscape. Its gilded window frames made the whole Hall glow through the heat of the sun. 'This is it Ruby, we've done it. We've made it to Journey's End and found Withinreach Hall where the Leisure Wizard lives. We'll be able to rest soon but let's have one more big push and get there as quickly as we can now.'

Tony was overjoyed at the thought of being so close to the Wizard and ran down the mountain with a huge smile of his face. As they got closer to the Hall though, his smile started to slip as if it was melting from his face in the heat of the day. He should have felt happy knowing that he was so near to the person who could tell him how to rescue his beloved Leisure Service but he couldn't help but feel unwelcome. He hadn't even reached the gates of the mansion before warning signs almost shouted out 'KEEP OFF THE GRASS', 'NO DOGS ALLOWED' and 'BALL GAMES STRICTLY PROHIBITED!'.

How silly, Tony thought. If we want to encourage people to enjoy an active lifestyle we should be inviting them onto the grass to kick a ball around with their friends. Tony also reflected on how much healthier he'd become since he'd had Ruby to take on walks or long runs like this one.

Withinreach Hall was surrounded by a black wrought iron fence decorated with gold highlights and scrollwork. It was the kind of fence that might be found around Buckingham Palace to help keep the Queen and all of her valuables safe. Tony wasn't surprised to find that the front door of Withinreach Hall was locked shut so he looked around for a door knocker or bell. On the wall at he side of the door was a buzzer with a small typed sign beneath which read 'Press for Attention'. Tony did as instructed and waited… and waited… and waited. Tony rang the bell again in case the person at the other end hadn't heard it and again he waited… and waited… and then he heard a faint click which sounded as if the door had just been unlocked. He pushed hard against the heavy looking door until it opened far enough for him and Ruby to squeeze through.

Once inside he was confronted by an imposing reception desk with a high laminate counter with thick glass screens above. It reminded Tony of the reception desks he had in some of his Leisure Centres that were built in the 1980's. It was the kind of desk that was designed to keep people out rather than welcome them in. Behind the glass he could see an elderly woman doing all she could to make herself look busy. She shuffled some papers and put them on a pile on one side of a desk. She then looked through the pile and pulled out a piece of paper and placed it on the other side of the desk. She picked up the phone but forgot who she was going to call and then she returned the single piece of paper back to the top of the pile on the other side of the desk. In all this time she hadn't looked up once to acknowledge Tony.

Perhaps she hasn't seen me, thought Tony, so moved up to the desk and placed his mouth as close as he could to the glass screen with a circle of dots cut into it beneath which was painted the words 'Speak Here'. He was just about to speak but was suddenly distracted by the sight of an owl on a perch at the far end of the reception desk. On the wall behind the owl hung what looked like a faded old certificate with a gold emblem in the bottom right hand corner. Eventually the words came. 'Excuse me', said Tony, but this didn't prompt a response. So, Tony raised his voice a little and called 'excuse me' which prompted an angry reply of 'I'll be with you in a minute, can't you see I'm busy?'

When the woman finally shuffled over to the counter Tony politely asked if he could see the Leisure Wizard. 'He's out,' she snapped, 'and he's too busy to see anyone'. 'I don't mind waiting' said Tony, 'I've come such a long way and would like to ask his advice'.
'As you please' said the woman, but you'll have a long wait. 'Go and sit over there' she said, pointing to some uncomfortable looking wooden chairs without cushions, 'and keep quiet while I'm working.'
Tony politely asked if there was somewhere he could get a drink for Ruby and himself but this just prompted another angry response. 'The vending machine is out of order and the engineer won't be here 'til next week, so you'll have to go without.'

'I wouldn't be happy if one of my receptionists spoke to a customer like that', whispered Tony to Ruby which drew a very loud 'shush' from the woman, as if Tony had just spoken out loud in a public library. Tony sat as still and as quietly as he could on the uncomfortable wooden chair for over an hour glad of the chance to rest his legs, while Ruby slept on the floor with her head cushioned on his slightly sore feet.

Without warning, the woman behind the counter shouted 'we're closing now so you'll have to leave'.
'I can't leave yet' said Tony, 'I haven't seen the Wizard'.
'Well that's just too bad' she said, 'now take your dog and get out'.
'I'm not going anywhere while you speak to me like that' snapped Tony, 'You have been very rude to me since I stepped foot through those doors and I am not leaving here until you've apologised and I have seen the Wizard'.
I'll call security and have you thrown out then,' said the woman 'and then you'll be banned from ever coming here again'.
'Go and call security then,' said Tony determined to stay put until he'd seen the Wizard.

Tony had obviously caused a commotion and could see the woman talking to someone in an adjoining room through a small crack in the door. Before he knew it, he was on his aching feet and had approached the counter where he caught a glimpse of a tiny bald headed man with round glasses using the door to try to shield himself from view. Tony had the vague feeling that he recognised the man as the Leisure Wizard from the web site. 'Excuse me,' he called, 'are you in charge here. I'd like a word with you and would like to complain about my treatment here today'.

The door suddenly snapped shut and stayed shut for what felt like a lifetime. Tony was determined to see someone if only to register his complaint and called out 'I'm not leaving until someone has the courtesy of speaking to me. I've travelled a very long way with my dog to get here to ask for advice and we'll stay here all night if we've got to.'

Reluctantly it seemed, the door cracked open and a tiny looking man in glasses peered through the gap at Tony. The door was slowly nudged open bit by bit until a tiny, bald headed man with round glasses, wearing a shabby old green suit and slippers shuffled forward and stood before them. His voice was timid and quivered as he introduced himself almost apologetically as the Leisure Wizard.

Tony had been expecting to meet somebody altogether more imposing than this but politely shook the man's hand whilst introducing himself and Ruby. 'I've been anticipating this moment for so long and had rather expected a much warmer welcome than the one we've just received, said Tony.
'I am so very sorry,' replied the Wizard, 'but my wife, Professor Prowler over there on his perch and I are no longer used to receiving visitors at Withinreach Hall and I'm afraid we seem to have forgotten our manners. Our customers, the ones we still have left, no longer visit us in person but prefer to contact us through the web-thingy these days so we rarely practice our customer contact skills. Now if you don't mind me asking, why have you come here?'

They sat together on the uncomfortable wooden seats while Tony explained the position for his beloved Leisure Service and the wonderful people who worked for him if he couldn't turn their fortunes around. He told the Wizard of his plans for future and of his difficulty in getting the people 'on the 5th floor' to share his vision. He talked with great enthusiasm about his plans before going on to explain how he had found his way to Withinreach Hall at Journeys End and of the people he had encountered along the way. His story captivated the Wizard who listened attentively throughout without speaking a word.

When finally the Wizard did speak he simply said 'so let me ask you again, why have you come here?'
'Why? To ask your advice on how I might reduce, or preferably eliminate the subsidy needed to run Leisure Services before the Council opts to hand it over to a private sector Health and Fitness provider.'
'Well it seems to me that you've already got all the answers you need', said the Wizard slightly mysteriously.
'It doesn't feel that way to me', said Tony, starting to feel sorry for himself.
'But as you recounted your journey to Withinreach Hall to me, you've just confirmed that you do have all the answers already. Isn't that right Professor Prowler?' he called across to his owl. 'He should know' the Wizard said to Tony. He's been keeping an eye on you since you and Ruby took your first steps on this journey. 'Let me recap your story for you and I'm sure that the answers you are looking for will become clearer.'

And with that, the Wizard led Tony step by step through each stage of his journey.

'The colourful Councillor Morgan took you to the Isle of Dosh to Show you his vision for Leisure. That was a nice move on his part. I always think it's a good idea to show people an example wherever possible. It helps people understand what you are trying to achieve. It helps them get the picture.'

'Councillor Morgan likes to make money, and there's nothing wrong with that, but his vision couldn't be further removed from the Healthy Living Agenda that you have to work to if he tried. He may be pleased to be cashing in on his 'punters' love of fast food and drink but experience warns us that there will be a heavy price to pay in future in terms of coronary heart disease, diabetes and obesity.'

'You are right to hold on to your vision to encourage everybody, young or old, to enjoy an active lifestyle. Good quality Leisure Centres that offer their customers affordable prices can have an important role in achieving this.'

'What you must do now, is share your vision – with Councillors, with Sandra Potts and other senior officers in the Council, with your staff, and most importantly, with your customers. Communication is key so use every means at your disposal to get your message heard. Improving health through physical activity is a compelling argument so shout about it. I'm sure that there will be a lot of people who will want to follow your lead.'

It was Tony's turn to be enthralled and he sat quietly taking in every word that the Wizard said.

'Now let's move on. Professor Prowler told me that you learned a lot on Tuppenceworth Moor.'

Tony shouldn't have been surprised to hear that the Leisure Wizard had spoken to his owl but still raised an eyebrow in disbelief. Catching the look that Tony had just given him the Wizard said, 'Oh yes, Professor Prowler has been watching your progress all along your journey. Don't you remember feeling like you were being watched as you walked on the boggy moor? That was the Professor over there watching every move you made and listening to every word that was spoken. He's told me all about your conversation with Norman Ellis. He even told me that you do a fine impersonation of Sandra Potts.'

'While we think about Ms Potts, let's remind ourselves what she said to you in the past. I believe she told you that you didn't have a business case. But what is a business case? It's simply a document that allows you to set out your vision and explain how you intend to achieve it. It gives you the chance to say why Leisure needs to change and the consequences for the service if it doesn't. Ms Potts is an accountant by trade and she will always pay particular attention to the financial projections that are being made for both income and expenditure.'

'Ms Potts has taught you a valuable lesson and it served you well in your encounter with Norman Ellis, a man who told you that he could tweak a business case he'd used before to meet your needs. Every business case is unique and you should feel proud at how well you put him in his place when you told him that neither you nor Sandra Potts would accept a tweaked business case.'

'His proposition of using private sector finance to redevelop your facilities is an interesting one though and lots of Council's throughout the country are now using this as an option. Many are also using the Invest to Save scheme that you suggested. Setting out each option in detail in your business case will help you compare the pros and cons of each which will help you select the option that best meets your needs.'

'Poor Mr Ellis was knocked completely off balance at your suggestion of sharing the financial risk with you if he felt so confident about his proposals. This was such an intelligent proposition from you and shows how you have matured as a financial manager. I'm sure that even the icy Ms Potts would thaw if you presented her with a well worked out proposal that not only shows her that you have considered all the options and the risks associated with them. This will increase her confidence in any recommendation that you make.'

'Any questions so far?' asked the Wizard. Tony was feeling proud with himself but also a little embarrassed at the praise he'd just received and simply shook his head allowing the Wizard the space to continue. 'Then let's look at what happened when you got to the market town of Shillingsgate.'

'Did you recognise Professor Prowler on the Early Bird marketing materials that Lucy showed you?'

Tony thought back and remembered the picture of the swooping owl that looked like it was about to catch the bargain of the century. 'That was Professor Prowler?' asked a bemused Tony who was beginning to feel that the Wizard has somehow orchestrated his journey to Withinreach Hall.

'That was indeed Professor Prowler', said the Wizard, and with Lucy's help he showed you and Pauline Carter that there is more to running a successful marketing campaign than buying a big banner. A marketing campaign has to be worked out in advance so that all the materials can be ready in time and so that the aims of the campaign can be explained to staff. Think how well Lucy explained the Early Bird promotion to you. Do you think she would have done so well without having a really good understanding of the promotion and her role within it? No, of course she wouldn't. How well have you briefed your staff on any promotion that you have run', asked the Wizard? This simple but pointed question pricked the bubble of pride that Tony had been floating in since the Wizard praised his performance with Norman Ellis and brought him down to earth with a sudden ego bruising bump'.
'I haven't really spent any time briefing staff', confessed Tony. 'I've just assumed that they would know what I wanted and would get on with it'.

Ignoring the embarrassment that Tony was clearly feeling the Wizard continued, saying, 'And Lucy wasn't in Shillingsgate Market by chance you know. The Leisure Centre Manager had sent her there knowing that the market would attract a lot of people. She had been asked to speak to a given number of people knowing that some would sign up for Leisure Card on the spot, while others would prefer to leave their phone number for someone to call them later. Another day, she may be asked to go somewhere else where there is the prospect of speaking to a lot of people.'

'But Lucy probably had a background in sales', said Tony meekly, 'she really was very good at her job. I haven't got anybody like her working for me.'

'I'm sure that you have got plenty of enthusiastic people who work for you that share your passion for Leisure, said the Wizard. What they may need though is the training that shows them how to sell the benefits of Leisure. If you want your staff to sell more Leisure Cards to help achieve your vision then you have to see that sales training is just as important as the lifesaving skills you teach to lifeguards or the customer care training you give to your reception staff.'

'So I might have people like Lucy that already work for me and I just don't know it yet,' said Tony. The Wizard gave a wry smile and directed a quick wink to Professor Prowler, pleased that the proverbial penny had just dropped for Tony.

'That's right' said the Wizard, 'they are just waiting for you to show them the lead.'

This moment of realisation filled Tony with such energy that he could barely wait to run home and start to outline his plans in a business case.

'But what do I have to do to convince Pauline Carter to think in a different way about Leisure?' asked Tony.

'Ah yes, Pauline Carter,' chuckled the Wizard. 'She's still rooted to the spot in Shillingsgate you know. Your response to her was so well pitched that she hasn't yet worked out how to respond. I'd suggest that you work with Pauline to develop your marketing requirements and set them out in your business case. She's seen for herself now how effective a well-defined Leisure marketing campaign can be and I'm sure that she will want some of your success to rub off on her. And don't forget, once your business case is approved, Sandra Potts will be keeping a beady eye on progress against your targets. The thought of Ms Potts looking over her shoulder will help to keep Pauline on track.'

'You are a good Manager,' said the Wizard. 'Now go home and start believing in your own abilities. Set out your vision in a well-constructed business case and you'll soon find that there are plenty of people who will want to help you achieve your ambitions. Now unless you've got any more questions, I am feeling rather tired and would like to retire.'

'I do have two more questions,' said Tony. You've advised me, and I dare say hundreds of other Leisure Managers before me, on how to run a successful business. This means attracting people to use your facilities by adopting a proactive friendly approach to customers, providing them with modern, attractive and welcoming facilities that they will want to use again and again. Please forgive me asking but, what has happened to your business? The fences and signs around Withinreach Hall are like barriers to warn off intruders. They almost shout KEEP OUT!'

'Then once inside, there are more barriers to be faced in the form of the imposing reception desk and the most unwelcoming receptionist I've ever met.'

And if that wasn't enough, it looks like Withinreach Hall has become a shadow of its former self and needs some investment.'

Tony's comments stung and the Wizards eyes filled with tears.

'As I said' replied the Wizard dejectedly, 'I'm tired and would like to retire. I've been advising Leisure Managers for more years than I care to remember but it's an industry that needs young people with fresh ideas who understand the benefits of technology. These days Managers can get all the advice they need at the click of a button. I've been overtaken by computers,' said the Wizard.

'That's not true,' said Tony. I've come a long way to see you in person and I'm sure that there are plenty of Managers just like me who are struggling to improve Leisure Services despite huge financial pressures. You've shown me how to go about doing it and I'm sure that others would welcome the benefit of your experience and advice.

'My second question is this,' said Tony. If I came to you and told you that my business needed to be re-energised to maximise the power of the internet and other technologies, what advice would you give me?'

'I'd tell you to invest in the kind of training that would enable you to harness the power of the internet and to invest in building an attractive web site. These things should be done alongside the development of a marketing strategy to draw people to your business. This should also include the development of 'apps' to be used on mobile phones and tablets so that your customers can access your business at any time in a modern fun way.'

As he spoke the Wizard realised that he had just outlined a business case that would refresh his business. And with that, his eyes brightened, his head lifted and he straightened his shoulders.

'Oh, you are a very wise young man Tony, said the Wizard. I should be practicing what I preach and I am so pleased you came to Withinreach Hall to remind me of this.' I feel as if my batteries are already recharging at the prospect of moving my business into the 21st Century where my advice can still be relevant.'

The two men sat chatting and sharing ideas for a couple of hours enjoying each other's company before Tony said that he would have to leave to find his way back home.

'Before you go, there's something I'd like you to have,' said the Wizard, and shuffled off into his office. When he returned he was carrying an official looking scroll of paper tied with a crimson ribbon. He asked Tony to stand for a moment. 'You've travelled a long way to search out my advice and in the spirit of friendship have been happy to share ideas with an old fool who had lost his way. Many years ago I founded the Guild of Leisure Directors, otherwise known as GoLD, to help Senior Leisure Managers share their ideas on best practice within the industry. GoLD was built on the principle of teaching and training those in the Leisure industry so that they may reach their full potential. You are clearly committed to the Leisure Industry and the people who work within it. You started out on your journey with the desire to learn how to improve your Leisure Centres and have found the wisdom along the way to teach an old Leisure Wizard a lesson or two. In recognition of your dedication and personal development I am pleased to award you with this certificate which welcomes you into the Guild of Leisure Directors.'

Tony was completely lost for words as the Wizard shook his hand and presented him with his certificate but the smile on his face showed how proud he was to receive the award.

Chapter 4 – Meeting the Wizard	
Learning Outcomes (the learner will)	**Assessment Criteria (the learner can)**
• Understand the importance of customer care in attracting new users and retaining existing customers.	• Identify good practice within a Leisure facility. • Explain the importance of good customer care on attracting new uses and retaining existing customers.
• Understand the interpersonal skills needed to in the customer service environment.	• Describe the key interpersonal skills and relate each to a given situation.
• Understand how Leisure facilities use ICT to maintain customer records and keep them safe.	• Describe the records kept to maintain customer safety. • Describe how records are used legitimately for promotional purposes for existing and potential new users. • Explain how Leisure facilities safely store data on customers.
• Have a basic understanding of the software packages used in Leisure facilities and how they are used to drive new business.	• Describe what information is held be Leisure facilities to keep customers safe. • Describe how retained data can be used legitimately for promotional purposes. • Provide an outline of the Data Protection regulations that Leisure facilities have to comply with.

Activities Linked to Chapter 4

1. Produce a mind map of the skills needed to work on the reception desk of a Leisure facility.
2. Describe how Leisure facilities maintain their customer records. What software packages do they use?
3. What interpersonal skills would you need to work on the reception desk of a Leisure facility?
4. What are the key customer service skills needed to work on the reception desk of a Leisure facility?

Chapter 5 – Going Home

'The Leisure industry is in good hands while we have people like you working in it, Tony. Use your wisdom well,' the Wizard said as he waved Tony and Ruby goodbye. 'Professor Prowler will make sure you get home safely but stay on the old gold road and you won't go wrong. Goodbye Tony and good luck'.

With Professor Prowler as his guide and Ruby running at his side, Tony set off on his journey home. As he climbed the mountainside from where he had first set eyes on Withinreach Hall, the old gold road started to glitter in the sunlight. He stopped to watch the dazzling spectacle playing out before him but almost immediately had to close his eyes to protect them from a searing golden burst of light.

Blinded by the light for a moment he was aware of a rhythmic buzzing in his ears. As he opened his eyes he thought he was back in his living room sitting in front of his TV. Confused, he closed his eyes and shook his head before slowly opening them again. This time he was certain that he was sitting in the armchair in his living room in front of his TV with Ruby sleeping across his feet. Had his journey to see the Leisure Wizard just been a dream, he asked himself.

A flashing light by his right hand helped him to identify that the buzzing noise that had helped to wake him was in fact his mobile phone announcing that he had received a new text message. The message read: Follow this link to the Leisure Wizard Website and get the latest updates from the Guild of Leisure Directors.

Reaching down to stroke Ruby's head and wake her, a scroll of paper tied with a crimson ribbon rolled from his lap onto the floor. The scroll was a certificate awarded to Tony by the Guild of Leisure Directors. In the bottom right hand corner was a gold emblem embossed with the letters GoLD.

'This is weird,' said Tony, maybe I'm still dreaming. I really should go to bed but I'm excited by the thought of what tomorrow will bring. Whatever happens though, I promise that I will take you for a run across the field's tomorrow night.'

www.ingramcontent.com/pod-product-compliance
Lightning Source LLC
Chambersburg PA
CBHW072300200526
45168CB00016B/2209